WHERE
MANY RIVERS
MEET

Poems by DAVID WHYTE

1 9 9 0

MANY RIVERS PRESS

LANGLEY, WASHINGTON

Some of these poems have appeared in magazines, newsletters and journals, including, *Annals of Earth, Blind Donkey, Resurgence, Seakayaker* and others.

Library of Congress Catalogue Number 89-92406

ISBN 0-9621524-1-2

This book is for Autumn,
and all the years of love and support.

CONTENTS

CONTENTS *[continued]*

C O N T E N T S *[continued]*

[1]

THE RIVER BEGINS

ENOUGH

Enough. These few words are enough.
If not these words, this breath.
If not this breath, this sitting here.

This opening to the life
we have refused
again and again
until now.

Until now.

IT IS NOT ENOUGH

It is not enough to know.
It is not enough to follow
the inward road conversing in secret.

It is not enough to see straight ahead,
to gaze at the unborn
thinking the silence belongs to you.

It is not enough to hear
even the tiniest edge of rain.

You must go to the place
where everything waits,
there, when you finally rest,
even one word will do,
one word or the palm of your hand
turning outward
in the gesture of gift.

And now we are truly afraid
to find the great silence
asking so little.

One word, one word only.

FAITH

I want to write about faith,
about the way the moon rises
over cold snow, night after night,

faithful even as it fades from fullness,
slowly becoming that last curving and impossible
slither of light before the final darkness.

But I have no faith myself
I refuse it the smallest entry.

Let this then, my small poem,
like a new moon, slender and barely open,
be the first prayer that opens me to faith.

MUSE

The words insistent, wishing to be said,
   I walk back to the house, find the room lit,
a woman illuminated, by a table with flowers,
   needle in hand, her long fingers threading the cloth
with dark red thread. She turns to look.

The house is quiet, the wind shivers behind me,
   there is a single drop of blood on her hand.

[II]

THE RIVERS TO THE SEA

WHERE MANY RIVERS MEET

All the water below me came from above.
All the clouds living in the mountains
gave it to the rivers
who gave it to the sea, which was their dying.

And so I float on cloud become water,
central sea surrounded by white mountains,
the water salt, once fresh,
cloud fall and stream rush, tree roots and tide bank
leading to the rivers mouths
and the mouths of the rivers sing into the sea,
the stories buried in the mountains
give out into the sea
and the sea remembers
and sings back
from the depths
where nothing is forgotten.

THE SEA

The pull is so strong we will not believe
the drawing tide is meant for us,
I mean the gift, the sea,
the place where all the rivers meet.

Easy to forget,
how the great receiving depth
untamed by what we need
needs only what will flow its way.

Easy to feel so far away
and the body so old
it might not even stand the touch.

But what would that be like
feeling the tide rise
out of the numbness inside
toward the place to which we go
washing over our worries of money,
the illusion of being ahead,
the grief of being behind,
our limbs young
rising from such a depth?

What would that be like
even in this century
driving toward work with the others,
moving down the roads
among the thousands swimming upstream,
as if growing toward arrival,
feeling the currents of the great desire,
carrying time toward tomorrow?

Tomorrow seen today, for itself,
the sea where all the rivers meet, unbound,
unbroken for a thousand miles, the surface
of a great silence, the movement of a moment
left completely to itself, to find ourselves adrift,
safe in our unknowing, our very own,
our great tide, our great receiving, our

wordless, fiery, unspoken,
hardly remembered, gift of true longing.

LOOKING OUT FROM LANGLEY

Saratoga Passage,
arm of grey water,
we cannot know you
as you know yourself.

But to us your flowing hand
is slowly opening between the islands
lifting its fingers to the white mountains.

Watching you,
our hands open also
and hold the railings as we lean toward your secret.

You open to us our own depths
from which, like the sea, we can never turn away.

But only the bronze statue
of the young boy dreaming can feel you as we should.
He rests his open eyes upon the mountain
sure in his silence that your world is his.

He knows what heals his immobility
and that is why he keeps you close,
locked forever in his metal heart.

TIME LEFT ALONE

The standing stones are silent, the ground will not speak,
the half-moon flares in a dark sky, locking them in shadow.
How many times, blindfold by time, staring out through starlight
or before dawn at the dreamless face of the sea about to wake
have young men entered the waves and left the shore-line forever.

Our fathers no longer speak of this or turn their lined faces
to walls white-washed by moon-light, seeing the same walls
their own fathers saw, hoping the same half-hopes, unable
to let time go, finding only as the needle's dropped in death
the breath's a thread pulled in and out of the present.

But tired of land we open ourselves to oceans, tired of time
we give back all that we've taken, tired of ourselves
we open ourselves to ourselves at last, sensing the waves
and great abyss of the sea beyond, the ocean stretching on sand
and the long view on the still sea that leads to another life.

And we go out as the fish go out, leaving the taste
of the rivers we know, joining the dark invisible weight
of what we would become, the calm sense of movement
seeing the others forming our shoals, and the scales
on our sides filling the depth with trembling stars.

In that depth, return's instinctual, the moon harvests
the long years and binds them in sheaves in a circle,
and we return too, for home from the sea we come to the river,
turning the ocean's face toward land, opening to silence
as the salmon opens to the sweet water in a saltless stream.

And out of the rivers we're taken again, returned to a land
we hardly remember, as out of memory we come to our senses
walking the cold night, this sea of blades stirred slightly
by a shifting breeze, this half-known need to know
what others hardly knew themselves, this silence in the stars

Leading to the dawn's first edge of sky and a silence
in ourselves that has no resolution. We would forget
if we could what all this meant, our fathers forgot
how giving up our need for time we join a greater time
and so these early years are years for growing old.

Older than our fathers could. To let time be alone
outside of what we need. To hold it where it's held in trust
beyond our need for time itself. Where the hand's grasp
opens in surprise and fear, to find itself full, and the face
that opens at last can see itself new, full in the depth of the sea.

THE SHAPES OF THE WORLD

Stooped low on the beach gathering firewood,
round, bleached and shaped by a gracious weather,
I find the eyes of mythical totems,
the shapes of fish and orca's fins.

My friend tends the fish, I tend the fire.
Slowly the fish fries in its round black pan.
Beneath, the innumerable shapes of other fish
salted by many years, burn blue and red and
yellow.

Our two kayaks are turned on a gravel beach,
steel grey light on their upturned bows,
while woodsmoke drifts out beyond them,
smudging the islands guarding the cove.

Through those small islands we coasted
skirting the wild weather chasing our sterns,
and I remember, that as we struck gravel
I felt the shape of things to come.

It was as if I remembered how all things fit
one to another and the sound of gravel
was the sound of home, and at the place where
water meets land I could meet all things.

On the cold beach we made a nest, a tent
shadowed by trees, a small fire, a place to sit.
The pure silence of honest work,
twigs cracking in the moist air.

Above us the young eagle circled
seeking a glimmer in the sea.
The waves murmered on the beach,
the gravel's voice rising and falling.

When we find a home like this
it must be that the old ones come by,
join us on the rough log seats,
throw their arms round our shoulders,

speak lovingly of the eagle,
laugh between mouthfuls of fish.
Tell us to go back, tell the old stories.
How the shapes of the world can speak.

WATCHING THE SUN GO DOWN

In the evening, that shadow on Coldspring
is where the sun goes down.
Time, when the bow touches shore, to watch
the sun roll down that long curve of hillside
and wait.

Paddle laid crossways,
back leaning on the upright seat,
heels resting in cold water,
rudder pulled up.

Time to feel the day long movement of the paddle
come to rest in tired arms,
to lift the spray-skirt, stand up,
keep the weight low,
step out of the boat
into the shallows.

Time to pull the kayak up the beach,
open the hatches, take out the tent,
turn the kayak over
on the rough grey drift-wood logs.

Time to say nothing, just watch
without moving, without sound,
the sun reflected, shimmering,

setting on fire
the white length of an upturned kayak.

SETTING OUT AT DUSK

The kayak sits on the black water
covered by trees.
Late October leaves drift by its bow.

Paddling out for weekend days away from noise
this silence leaves me unsure,
an old friend I haven't met for years.

I sit, rudder pulled up, getting to know him,
double bladed paddle
dipping slowly in cold water

and looking up, see a single otter, skittering
on the grassy bank, stop,
look round, see me, low shape on still water,

roll back into the trees, leave me with silence.
I watch clouds gather between islands,
the wind pick up, shearwaters lift on the grey sea.

Through the sip-slap of waves on the lifting hull
I prick my ears for the small sounds
at the very edge of silence and then

I pull the bow out into the wide sea
paddle dipping
toward darkness and enter again. The quiet.

SONG FOR THE SALMON

For too many days now I have not written of the sea,
nor the rivers, nor the shifting currents
we find between the islands.

For too many nights now I have not imagined the salmon
threading the dark streams of reflected stars,
nor have I dreamt of his longing
nor the lithe swing of his tail toward dawn.

I have not given myself to the depth to which he goes,
to the cargoes of crystal water, cold with salt,
nor the enormous plains of ocean swaying beneath the moon.

I have not felt the lifted arms of the ocean
opening its white hands on the seashore,
nor the salted wind, whole and healthy
filling the chest with living air.

I have not heard those waves
fallen out of heaven onto earth,
nor the tumult of sound and the satisfaction
of a thousand miles of ocean
giving up its strength on the sand.

But now I have spoken of that great sea,
the ocean of longing shifts through me,
the blessed inner star of navigation
moves in the dark sky above
and I am ready like the young salmon
to leave his river, blessed with hunger
for a great journey on the drawing tide.

[III]

THE RIVERS IN THE MOUNTAINS

KATHMANDU

Because I am tired
                and have
wasted all day in the city,
I decide to sit and
the luminous sky sits also
and fills my busy hands with calm.

The white concrete
like a high cliff above me
watches me sit
at the small table
with my white cup and black tea,
and like one of those pilgrims
who arrive at last
at the dark mountain lake,
I have found it.

And as if drawn to quiet
and the high mountains to which we go,
the mouth slips through steam
ready to drink,
alive, unspeaking,
from the black silence
at the water's edge.

MUKTINATH

Dawn at Muktinath
and I look through the window,
white mountains and the steady
slopes of snow,
cold scent of pine and the raven-call
of black birds
circling upward - toward nothing.

So the breath escapes the mouth
spiralling in a cold room,
so the words leave our lips,
the first line of a long poem
with no courage to finish.

This is the place the path begins,
the empty room beneath the breath
where everything we've broken
comes back to be repaired,
where bitterness returns, opens,
turns to a final sourness
on the lime-washed walls
and disappears.

This is the place we start again,
place sunburnt knuckles in moist eyes
and bow the head
feel the rough cold wall
on the forehead and weep.

This is the place we stop,
look up, lean out the window
and find the first signs of life.

Beneath us
a child is crying,
while above,
a tight arrow of driven ponies
points the way to the high pass.

TILICHO LAKE

In this high place
   it is as simple as this,
      leave everything you know behind.

Step toward the cold surface,
   say the old prayer of rough love
   and open both arms.

Those who come with empty hands
   will stare into the lake astonished,
   there, in the cold light
      reflecting pure snow

      the true shape of your own face.

SONG OF ONE WHO GOES ON
Above Manang

What I have left behind
has not left me.
Those I have failed
have not failed me,
and those I have not loved
will love me
even in my worst.

What I have not seen
or failed to see
I leave as gift.

The lands I have not walked
will offer their paths as I sleep.
This earth I have not loved
will hold me
even as I am laid beneath it.

To everything that is
I give everything I am not.

To the life through which
I have walked blindfold,
I give it the sight of my weakness.

To life I give thanks for this:-
one strength through great failure
with marvellous opportunity for all.

THE FACES AT BRAGA

In monastery darkness
by the light of one flashlight
the old shrine room waits in silence.

While above the door
we see the terrible figure,
fierce eyes demanding. "Will you step through?"

And the old monk leads us,
bent back nudging blackness
prayer beads in the hand that beckons.

We light the butter lamps
and bow, eyes blinking in the
pungent smoke, look up without a word,

see faces in meditation,
a hundred faces carved above,
eye lines wrinkled in the hand held light.

Such love in solid wood!
Taken from the hillsides and carved in silence
they have the vibrant stillness of those who made them.

Engulfed by the past
they have been neglected, but through
smoke and darkness they are like the flowers

we have seen growing
through the dust of eroded slopes,
their slowly opening faces turned toward the mountain.

Carved in devotion
their eyes have softened through age
and their mouths curve through delight of the carvers hand.

If only our own faces
would allow the invisible carver's hand
to bring the deep grain of love to the surface.

If only we knew
as the carver knew, how the flaws
in the wood led his searching chisel to the very core,

we would smile too
and not need faces immobilized
by fear and the weight of things undone.

When we fight with our failing
we ignore the entrance to the shrine itself
and wrestle with the guardian, fierce figure on the side of good.

And as we fight
our eyes are hooded with grief
and our mouths are dry with pain.

If only we could give ourselves
to the blows of the carvers hands,
the lines in our faces would be the trace lines of rivers

feeding the sea
where voices meet, praising the features
of the mountain and the cloud and the sky.

Our faces would fall away
until we, growing younger toward death
every day, would gather all our flaws in celebration

to merge with them perfectly,
impossibly, wedded to our essence,
full of silence from the carver's hands.

DREAMING AT BRAGA

Two miles to go and the door will open,
-three old men round an open fire.
One offers rice and one offers *dahl*
and the third asks fiercely
with empty hands,
"Oh which, traveller, is the true I?"

BED BUGS IN KAGBENI

Cold morning on a strange bed,
suddenly I am not alone!
Sharing the warmth inside my sleeping bag
there are small beings!
And I, lovingly, like Avolokitesvara
great bodisattva of compassion
gaze down upon them.
Strange heads and many legs!
Sharp and searching horns for human hair!

At times like this we abandon our search for meaning,
take the bag outside, hang it on the high wall,
inside out, look at the mountain, high snow
reflecting pure light all down the valley, onto the bag.

Go inside, wash, drink hot tea with salt
and small spots of yak butter.
Eat flat breads baked in pine-ash,
come out refreshed.
Take the bag, now unpopulated, in both hands,
lift it to the nose.
Fragrance of new morning!

Pack it away, go out the doors with friends
who also shared the night with others.
Ask how they slept,
laugh,
on the steep road to Jarkhot.

A WOMAN'S VOICE

Night at Latamarang.
Above the river and call of cicadas
I remember old words and old bonds
and beneath the singing of a woman's voice
the sight of my mother's face.

How strange to have forgotten!
The young boy with eyes wide,
the woman's cheek so close,
the small hand held up to be taken,
the yearning filled, the sun-warmed sky,
the mountain solid, immovable,
even here in the Himalaya
a thousand Buddhas of compassion
carved in the steep rocks above
bow down before the mother-love.

The teaching came with me,
the cicadas stop their calling,
the starry sky has turned to calm,
the river runs in the steep valley
to the dry lands and the waiting sea,

Years ago now I remember
I put away that guiding hand
to find the way myself
and find, strange wonder,
at journey's end
the self-same hand again.

LAST PASS BEFORE THE LOWLANDS

Through the steep valley
of pine woods and high rocks
we follow the path into silence.

Thick beds of
needles quieten our steps.
Pine and wild roses sweeten the air.

Mist whitens
the ridges and thoughts
turn to the things we left.

At a curve in the path
far above the falling river
we see the valley leading down.

White ridges
folding their edges
round a green nest of woodland,

and like a
breath the breeze
speaks of those who live below.

A sense of
going down now.
Away from the snow

the high pass
dry air and keen wind of Manang.
Over the white river a narrow bridge

and beyond it
the path curves again
to a small house on a rocky point

-wavering light
in the still air. We stop,
sit on the dry ground, look back

before mist
takes the pass, go down,
follow the path above the river

between the rocks
across the bridge, under the cliff.
After the pass, this house, warm air and the lowlands.

After
the first step home,
there is one return and no other.

[IV]

THE RIVERS OF LOSS

THE TEST

For Joel Comeaux.

How will you meet the demon of ignorance?

I will enter the church and go to the altar
and kneel in my bridal gown.

and there in my grief I will wait and wait
for the touch of his hand in mine.

He will not fail to come.

THE WELL OF GRIEF

Those who will not slip beneath
    the still surface on the well of grief

turning downward through its black water
    to the place we cannot breathe

will never know the source from which we drink,
    the secret water, cold and clear,

nor find in the darkness glimmering
    the small round coins
        thrown by those who wished for something else.

WAKING

Get up from your bed,
go out from your house,
follow the path you know so well,
so well that you now see nothing
and hear nothing
unless something can cry loudly to you,
and for you it seems
even then
no cry is louder than yours
and in your own darkness
cries have gone unheard
as long as you can remember.

These are hard paths we tread
but they are green
and lined with leaf mould
and we must love their contours
as we love the body branching
with its veins and tunnels of dark earth.

I know that sometimes
your body is hard like a stone
on a path that storms break over,
embedded deeply
into that something that you think is you,
and you will not move
while the voice all around
tears the air
and fills the sky with jagged light.

But sometimes unawares
those sounds seem to descend
as if kneeling down into you
and you listen strangely caught
as the terrible voice moving closer
halts,
and in the silence
now arriving
whispers

Get up, I depend
on you utterly.
Everything you need
you had
the moment before
you were born.

WHAT IS IT LIKE?

What is it like to be alone?
To fall into the abyss
where voices do not speak?

What is it like to have
given everything away?
In the *wrong* way?

What is it like to love no one?
To live in a house
shared only by servants?

What is it like?

It is like this.
You are alone beneath a cold moon,
you cannot speak,
the bitter night has pierced your clothes
and when you sleep
your body stirs with a chill wind
which hour after hour
and against your will
refuses to stop.

In the cold morning
you will be open
to one comfort only.

The barely conceived surprise
of being shaken awake.

ACTAEON TELLS ALL

I saw a stag through mist, silver,
fleeing from dogs through deep grass and meadow
then back under canopies of cool wood.

Saw her, pale light leaving the water,
lean down, lay her hair over green moss,
while above the legs curving, rising,

I saw a dark place, and the limp arms as if dead
lifted by the ones who bathed her.
Saw her tongue delirious in her open mouth

and small drops of water fall, linger
on the flesh rubbed pink.
Felt myself move unknowing forward,

and sense the strange energy that could
come between us were I to lie on her.
The night inside night and the first dream

at first touch. Snow drifting on white hills
and my warm hands where her secret lies.
Her eyes would leap fire I thought,

but she saw me first, made *me* burn, rear up
from her transformed, brown hooved in sudden leap,
nostrils flared in terror of the distant hounds.

I, now far from her, found a place to rest at last,
because all day between oaks I ran here
with strange horns, gave everything to her,
was bitten, brought down, eaten by my own dogs.

AFTER READING "POOR PEOPLE"
BY LIAM O'FLAHERTY

Snow in Vermont,
the bus along the grey road
enormous, eating up the distance to arrival.

Having read the story
how the child died, their only child
I too travel on long roads toward darkness.

They knelt by his bed
worn by poverty, broken by want
yet whole in their hurt and dispair.

Only the long hours
of loss to come, only the hand every day
opening the door to the house of grief.

In the misted window
I see my own son. If I should lose him now
could I go too into the black mouth of loss?

Last night I dreamt
he brought himself upright
his small legs wavering, then fell again.

A strange fall
as if I could not reach
the place where he might go.

But another rose
like a white statue on weak knees
arms lifted for my arms to catch.

His small arms
made mine feel strong.
How hard they held onto life!

I gave him
that fierce look
that knows of love but cannot speak.

And in the dream
he whispered. "Life loses hold,
but death is a friend to life."

I said. "One fell but another rose
though I live in fear
my hands are open for ever."

JOHN CLARE'S MADNESS

Northhamptonshire's
deadly flat
spreads beneath the hawk.

Watching hedgerows
and the muddy lanes.
Sharp eyed for winter he's aware again

how each small movement's plain
to the eye awake
for food or touch of rain

to make his feathers start.
My pen touched paper
just the same. Alert to follow

exactly what I saw. Said
exactly how I speak.
Now,

Northborough's
fields hold nothing,
-my house an empty shell.

Above Helpstone
the hawk circles
the house that I have failed.

There is a small body
caught in his claws,
it cries to the hawk in fear.

I said, beat, beat, strange wings,
what is won then lost
comes back with the fiercest pain.

FALLING FORWARD

Our breath rising in the cold air
we listen to his voice,
not hearing the words he speaks
nor seeing how closely
his eyes are pressed
now the news escapes his lips.

We turn away and walk
the grey sky filled with rain,
the path toward the gate darkening,
the throat aching to speak
and the old road beyond
curving toward home.

Strange to think I heard the words
only when I reached the gate
and felt the slow rain on my face
like a first terrible creation
as if waking underwater
unable to breath.
"Jonathan died an hour ago."

Stranger still to fall forward
holding the cold iron bars
my old invulnerable way in the world
turning at last into loss.

And there, amazed by what pulls us on
as the gate swung slowly open
I hung powerless, saying nothing
holding the bars
dragged into grief by my own weight.

NEWS OF DEATH

For Tom Charlotte

Last night they came with news of death
not knowing what I would say.

I wanted to say,
"The green wind is running through the fields
making the grass lie flat."

I wanted to say,
"The apple blossom flakes like ash
covering the orchard wall."

I wanted to say,
"the fish float belly up in the slow stream,
stepping stones to the dead."

They asked if I would sleep that night,
I said I did not know.

For this loss I could not speak,
the tongue lay idle in a great darkness,
the heart was strangely open,
the moon had gone,
and it was then
when I said, "He is no longer here",
that the night put its arm around me
and all the white stars turned bitter with grief.

THE MASK OF DEATH

From the hospital bed
you look back on the world of life
and already the only words you speak
are the ones rehearsed by heart.

And the face rising
from the white sheets around your feet
is the face for which you have waited.
Its lips are strong and its eyes are empty
and the cheek bones are dark and still.

It is the face of all you have not known
staring through the strange hollow inside you
that refused before to know the pain.

Yes you are chilled
and the small child you were a moment before
slips his frightened eyes beneath the sheets.

But with the small gesture of love
that is left to you,
slip your left arm around the frail child's shoulder
and with the other
raise yourself slowly toward those eyes.

And when you feel through the distance
that cannot make you falter
the bones of his cheeks as yours
and your empty eyes turn inward
on the griefs you would not know

you will want no other vision
and find, on your own lips
the first smile on the face of death
that will lead you to your joy.

VISION ON THE HILLS

That full view of the world seen as a child,
barely understood, a flight of half-remembered doves
and red leaves in violent rustle from the wind that followed.

Stone walls climbed the hilltops through thunder
and sleeting rain, entering the mist that drew me on
paths where every stone stood single, opening like eyes

to other worlds, the black-faced sheep snaking
out of moss and the stone-barns buttressed by
old stones and an older time to which I knew,

by seeing this, by seeing *now,* belonged to me
as I to them, welded by the heat of full attention
sustained by time, held up for all by youth

too caught in the ordinary
miracle to worry what was past
and what was present, or beyond it

whether the bright vision itself could fade.
It could, it did. It seems we slide down the long
curve of years falling through time until we wake

or dream like this: the window open
to find us, brazen miracle
momentary fresh, before we lose our faith again.

almost desperate, searching through the crowded years
we meet ourselves a final time, try to touch him,
hold him by the shoulders, teach us how to see again.

Our hands climb bewildered to our eyes,
too late we see everything, we ask everything
Who lost that vision? Who? Who lost that vision?

[v]

THE RIVERS OF THE SOUTH

PISAC, PERU

I remember those trees along the water,
a silent sky of clouds
in the river beneath their roots.

I remember you walking
and that silence on the bridge
asking us to stop.

I remember it like this
as if it will happen again,

above water, on a bridge
between two banks,
your dark hair and fierce eyes,

your refusal to go on
and your refusal to give up.

I remember it like this,
and then,
as you begin to speak,
my memory sees only the river
and your face
beneath a pale sky,
flowing away, as if forever.

HUARAS

Those mountains out of my past,
Cordillera Blanca,
blue snow and grey peaks
and a cold wind on the frigid lake.

The calmness in your eyes
for once without fear
for what it might mean
to be together
travelling south through Peru.

I remember you looked up
as if there might be promise
in something I might say or do.

Your face caught in sunlight
before the momentary cloud
darkened you again.

Above us the storm clouds
gathered everything
greedily,
leaving nothing to say.

Only when the clouds rolled
madly on the grey slopes
and we ran in the thunder
did I take your arm
speaking too quickly
what needed to be said.

Ten years later and I still
don't understand your answer,
and like then, after the storm,
we are still walking together,
two solitaries
moving slowly apart in the falling rain.

AYACUCHO

A cold wind off the mountain
as the grey light lies flat
on the ground where we walk.

Whoever looks back on this time
will only see two people
united in misunderstanding.

I know you will say this
is not so, there were other
darker compunctions
which held us truly
together.

There was the secret
we shared between us
which you would speak
and I would ignore.

There was the line upon line
of blue ridge and ochre mountain,
the dizzy field lines
tipped crazily toward the sky,
the patchworks of tilled earth
and memory
and the bitter Andean earth.
turning slowly under
the foot hoe.

In our love of bitterness
we seemed to drink that earth.
Its cold black heart filled
with an old sorrow.
Like the young girl in rags
in a sleet-storm of snow
following the sheep
off the hillside.

You asked me not to give
her anything.
I gave it anyway
and you raged
all the way into evening.
It made things worse
you said, as if we could
do something.

Now we look back
there *was* nothing we could do.
She turned into the snow
like someone
moving toward her own ghost.

And now we are all
together again,
you are here,
and she is here,
her cold knuckles
holding her shawl.
She is the one I am glad to see.
And you,
you will not get one word from me.

CUZCO

It became clear
toward evening.
The gold hands
of the high mountains
in a blaze from
the hidden sun,
the streaming light
and the shadows
in the west
hiding the nested
houses.
The train whistle
streaming
copper-colored smoke
as it left
through the fields
toward Puno.

You would stay
and I would go on.
One story already
becoming old,
how I left you.

Centuries gone by
and the tale will only
get better.
I left by train
to Bolivia,
flew to the north.
from La Paz

Now the fields
are passing
by the window
and the young men
turn toward home.
I remember your face
last night
close to mine,
looking down
on the cobbled streets,
you were a young girl
almost
wanting to begin again.

And I laughed
with you,
a wild faithlessness
to life
gripping me
for a moment.
It could have been
so easy,
one more day
true to the old promise
holding the tide of night at bay.

Who wrote this story
that we should meet
and part again?

The indifferent god
we had made ourselves,
faithless as ever to lovers
with plans.

MACCHU PICCHU

This sense of looking down
through green jungle
from the edge of a world
we had chosen together.

As if here, toward evening
we would know
how to leave
finally and forever
all the things
we had *not* chosen.

I remember your hair
and the dark-ridged slopes
of the mountains
flowing together.
The river
thousands of feet
below tumbling
toward dark.

I remember your look
of surprise as you
saw me, a stranger again.
Like the first time
looking up from the ocean
you called me by name.

And then, as if
we make meaning
simply in order
to leave it.

We forgot
everything,
looking out
from the mountain
over the walls
of centuries

the vanishing point
of the sun
extinguishing time
forever
to the instant
before we had met.

[VI]

THE RIVERS OF BRITAIN

THERE ARE THOSE

There are those we know
buried
not far beneath this green land
with whom
we have not spoken for a long time
who remember
what we have forgotten.

One day they will speak again
surprised at their own voices
singing the old song,
how the earth is given and taken
how the world will come again.

And we who also listen surprised
will come again to the land of lands.
Our own, the place we've chosen,
after the false start
and the slouching toward
falseness.

And find ourselves on the old roads
but new, walking with Blake, head up,
toward Jerusalem.

FIRST STEPS IN HAWKSHEAD CHURCHYARD

My son strode out into the world today,
twenty one steps on the grave of Ann Braithwaite,
her horizontal slab of repose grey beneath
the lifting red socks, her exit from the world
his entrance to the world of walking.

She must have lain beneath and smiled past
the small arms outstretched to the church tower of Hawkshead,
she must have borne him up, her help from the end of life
his beginning, her hands invisible, reaching to his.

He walked through each line explaining her life,
sixty two years by the small lake of Esthwaite,
lichen, green grass, grey walls and the falling
water of ice cold streams, his small place of play
her mingling with the elements she lived with.

A meeting of two waters,
hers a deep pool, solitary in stillness,
his swift, bubbling from rock to rock,
pouring into her silence, a kingfisher
flare in her darkness, promise of light,

Ineffable, unknowable, the touch of his feet
a promise of a world to come, solid on a life well lived.
His look of surprise when the church bell rang, her knowing.
The sound of time, his now, hers then. New rituals
are always played on the graves of those long dead.

OWL CALLS

Late evening in Esthwaite and the half-moon rides
above a still lake of clouds. Only the white sweep
of car lights curving through hedgerows, only the mind
coming to rest in tired arms, leaning on the rough wood gate.

Falling in with silence and the quiet appearance
of owls gliding toward woodland. Only the dark bulk
of cows to be heard cropping the fresh wet grass
and the still water color sky washed above the eyes.

The first whispering of an old poem, long memorized,
each line outlined by quiet. The young boy
blowing in his fists to call the owls, baffled by silence,
uncertain, unsure of what he called.

The owl's voice returned, the long silence,
the mouth open in surprise as if to speak,
and even now I sense the first faint crawl of his skin
and shiver of cold, as in that same moment, empty of sound,
the scarlet break-lights flare between trees and are gone.

COTSWOLD

A sandstone grave crowding shellfish,
fossils crusted round a copper plaque.

A silent church and an old house
and small green lines explaining grief.

The quiet rivulets of centuries
the stone green moss of years gone by,

the green hillsides, stone gold walls, shadows,
the buried pathways in the quiet wood.

Water falling enlivens, greens,
soaks and comes together underground.

Earth rising meets, moulds, holds,
holds on to what it owns, takes back

nothing not given. Over the shoals
of leaves and humus, over the branch

of oak and hedgerow, over the white aproned
hawthorn holding her skirts in the wind,

in the still moments before the wind shivers
across the still reflection on the moss rimmed pond

the white clouded sky is sailing as ever
over the rook-nests in the eastern woods.

And this lane that I follow burying through
greensward and the grey limbs of trees,

shadowing the rutted track into silence
is no place to speak. Now for years gone by

this entanglement of green has grown to
this moment's walking as if to measure

my readiness for quiet. Where I've failed
before now my body's alive to enter the silent

reflection of water from last night's rain
filling the wheel tracks in the muddy lane.

Walking the roads is enough today,
I'll follow the dark line of receding sun

over by Edgeworth, drop down, keep to the hedgerows,
speak only to myself, find myself speechless

at the edge of night. Composing clear lines,
-everything I've seen the tongue can tell.

HARTSHEAD

In Hartshead I'm walking paths I've walked for years
following the line of trees through wind, rain

and dark clouds moving fast from the moors. I've learned
to know since young the faint path through the fields

that takes you to the woods, above the valley,
leads you through hedgerows spiked with haws.

And still between those trees I see Huddersfield
cramped in the Colne, Castle Hill, the westering line

of Saddleworth Moor smouldering above. Winter's bleak
but still there's the green armchair of the valley sheltered

by wood and the pale green fields worked from the farm.
In snow, there's a sharp edge to the eye's inventory of

stonewall and hedgerow, a white silence stretched to breaking
on the still days the wind begs off from the west.

Spring's an apple green, bladed with new grass and blackened
with cows turned out from the barns. The hawthorn's white

surprise still shocks the eye's forgetful winter rest. Summer's
a still image. Shimmering heat and the streaked blurr of a rabbit

out from the gorse on Hartshead lane. The road a parched wander
to liquid, waist-high green-gold barley foresting the path

to the Grey Ox Inn. Now Autumn's the damped fire of fallen leaves
raked over by wind, the earthly crackle of bracken underfoot,

the giver of vision, the light defined by dark, the firm upward needle
of Clifton spire flared by a single ray from the clouds.

TAN-Y-GARTH

Elegy for Michael

This grass-grown hill's a patchwork lined with walls
I've grown to love. Four hundred years at least the

hill farm's clung tenacious to the weathered slope
over the Ogwen and the green depths of Mon.

The eye has weathered also, into the grey rocks
and the fields bright with spring, the wind blown light

from the mountains filling the valley,
the low backed sheep following the slope

hemmed by the dogs and John's crooked staff, the still valley
filled with his shouts and the mewling of sheep pressed

through the gate. Beneath Yr Elen, the bowl of Llafer's
stirred with mist, the dogs lie low in the tufted grass and

watch with pure intent the ragged back of the last sheep
entering the stone-bound pen. The rough ground of Wales

lives in the mind for years, springing moor grass under
feet treading concrete, hundreds of miles from home,

and the ground has names, songs full of grief, sounds
that belong to a single stream, Caseg's the place of the mare,

Cwm Llafer's the valley of speech, utterance of wind,
Fryddlas the blue moorland filled by the sky. The farm

passed down but never possessed lives father to son
life after life, feeding the sheep with grass,

the people with sheep and memory with years
lived looking at mountains. One single glance of a hillside

darkened by cloud is enough to sense the world it breathes
and the names need all the breath we have.

Carnedd Llewellyn, Carnedd Dafydd, Garnedd Uchaf, all the
Carneddau, Yr Elen of the shining light, Drosgl the endless

ridge curving to nothing. One man I know loved this place so
much he said he'd found his place to die. Years I knew him

here walking the high moor lines or watching the coals
of a winter fire in the cottage grate. And die he did but not

before one month's final joy in wild creation gave him that
full sight he'd glimpsed in Blake, he too struggled with his angel,

in and out of hospital, the white sheets and clouds unfolded
to the mountain's bracing sense of space, now he was ready,

his heart so long at the edge of the nest shook its
wings and flew into the hills he loved. Became the hills

he loved. Walked with an easy rest cradled by the faith he
nursed for years in doubt. His ashes are scattered over by

Aber, the water continually saying his name, as I still go
home to Tan-y-Garth speaking the names of those I know.

THE OLD TRADITION

Under the oak of the druid
we wait by the stream at Cwm Buchan.
Discovering its shadows and silence,
its secret falling water
turning toward night.

And deeper even than the stillness of night
is this quiet, now given over to water,
the faint whisper of rising wind
and the first rustle of leaves on the oak.

Here we study the old tradition
- giving up what was never possessed.

Here we run our fingers along the sharp
strange edge of silence
feeling the blade that cuts away the self.

And the man I was, just a moment before
is also there in the silence, cupping his hands,
drinking deep draughts with the thirst
of one who is wounded.

My voice insistent, I startle him.
"Stop drinking,
I forgive you your selfish life."

One astonished moment of surprise
then the cupped reflection
swaying beneath his face
slips between the interwoven fingers
drops to the surface and dies.

EASTER MORNING IN WALES

A garden inside me, unknown, secret,
neglected for years,
the layers of its soil deep and thick.
Trees in the corners with branching arms
and the tangled briars like broken nets.

Sunrise through the misted orchard,
morning sun turns silver on the pointed twigs.
I have woken from the sleep of ages and I am not sure
if I am really seeing, or dreaming,
or simply astonished
walking toward sunrise
to have stumbled into the garden
where the stone was rolled from the tomb of longing.

⌐VII⌐

RIVERS FROM A FORGOTTEN COUNTRY

HANDS ACROSS THE WATER

Impossible to write about Ireland:-
the blood's entangled and the heart won't go
where others went before me
shaking their swords and their pens at the moon.

Whatever brought my mother to England
banished her son to the dark glass of distance.

I remember cards from the family:-
and the well formed lines
"Hands across the water."

Marvellous cliché worth singing again!
and I harbored those words
as a wry link with home.

Now I know the short-cropped grass
on the high Reeks of Kerry,
the cold grey water
in the Blasket Sound.

And down at the Mile Post
out of Waterford town,
my great-uncle Davy,
coming to meet,
ducking and weaving,
arms flexed in a boxer's crook.

"Did you see the fight last night?
The best in all my years;
they stood there,
fist to fist,
arm to arm,
knee to knee,
and toe to toe
and by God,
they murdered one another."

Hands across the water
well enough;
but now I'm forever
wrapped in its arms
crouched,
trying to break,
shielding my face
from the welcoming blows.

RETURN

The day started with a flurry of gulls
and a single cry, as if I had spoken
and out of the deep cave where my tongue lies
birds were scattering in an open sky.

I went to the rail and watched them rise
over the grey clouds as if the sky were a sea
and the sea was cold now, full of shapes
and the horse-tails of winter.

And I spoke, involuntary
out of a delighted mouth
the old, strange word

Ireland;
joy when uttered, grief when heard.

SPIDDAL HARBOUR

It is night.
Three fishermen
treading softly
on the cool wet stones
carry a tray of shining fish.

The youngest stops,
looks out to sea
murmurs in a low voice
while the others pull him on.

"I am sick of this life,
I should have gone with Michael
- to America."

They will not look at him
they will not turn,
but the moon looks at him
and the fish
with each, silver, upturned eye.

IN A MOMENT OF MADNESS,
A DUBLIN POET THINKS OF
AN OLD LOVE

Twenty years since I knew her.
Wherever she is now, I will go to her.
I know you can never believe me
but her face is as fresh to me
as the winter day we parted.

Once my life was like a flight
through clear air, searching the field lines
for a high place from which to see.
Now, they have clipped my wings
turned my proud eagle flight
into the hesitant perching of a shivering wren.

It is in the shape of my old self then,
the hawk, the curlew, or anything wild
that flies against the sky
that I'll find her once again
staring out from the woods
on a winter evening.

Like this then,
as a soundless shadow of love
I will fly to the low branch above her.

HOW THE ROCKS
CAME TO IRELAND

Today on the cliff
as if walking through cloud,
seeing turf and stone walls
and the wet road through Clare,
the land opened up an old door again.

Grey rocks circled up the cliffs
dancing and falling.

Mounds of ice scoured off the land,
blinding my eyes.

Then cold, a scent of rough water,
and open sea where land had been.

Between waves now, shoulders rising,
the rocks push ashore,
black, forbidding, fathers of all.

Round their green dripping waists
the sea birds scream
and the sea breaks hammering their sides.

And the land says.
Forget the old stories?

Impossible!

-How the rocks came to Ireland.

SEEKING OUT TIME

In Ireland, Time has never been understood.
Each day under brooding clouds
the rocks come ashore on the coast of Clare.
They find Time, a silhouette, dark and indistinct,
a black bird perching in the hedgerows.

They seek Time out, want to know what he's doing,
why history lies thick on the ground
like braided rope, gold, satin,
wound with the blood of men and women,
tight knots choking the first spring grass.

Time stays at a distance, but they move closer.
His song whistles as if from a cave
whose entrance is Clouds-parting.
His yellow beak catches the sun
and his black feathers turn blue in the changing light.

Time goes mute, they are rocks from the sea,
unknown, forbidding, before Time.
His eyes smoulder, their small veins branching,
filling with blood. Why should rocks come ashore?

Time takes off, begins to creep
his wings across the hills, makes darkness
all day long, a sky of feathers on which,
head tilted sideways, his eye becomes a strange moon.

They shake their fists, threaten him,
but Time has risen, covered in twilight
like dust, no one can touch him.

Time sends down mist, chaos by night, startled curses,
screams that appear from their own throats.
"Time is afraid" they taunt.
Time says. "I am friends with no one."

He will not come down. They began to sing.
Slowly they form in a circle and slowly
they chant the song of the shoreline,
filling the cave of his wings with sound.
Bringing Time down.

Slowly he descends and slowly he curves in the song.
The breeze softens his feathers,
his eyes glaze toward the prison at their center.

Time comes down, stoops right in their center.
His beak curves to the brown earth,
when it touches, his eyes flash fire, cold and clear.
Time leaves Ireland, disappears and leaves them,
frozen, standing stones on the bare hill.

POEM IN PRAISE OF THE TRINITY HARP

For Peter Kilroy

Rough barked, walnut brown, milky darkness,
shaped like a wind blown tree,
etched and hieroglyphed, a calligraphy of shapes and love.

Three branches of willow
held together by strong arms
invisible inside the wood, waiting for other arms.

Worn, round, rubbed where the left arm stretched down
and where the eye descends we find below
low, where the right arm touched, this valley of use,

glen of embracement, erotic hollow of summer delight.
Here the crooked arm held,
here the sounds like small green buds, grew into leaf,

rustled with wind, filled with sound from the western sea
a dark forest of notes rushing inland
to the fields, filling the heartland of Ireland.

And this tree leans, the whole tree leans in the wind
of centuries, swayed by time and the downward
pull of brass, gold sinews snapping between opposites.

Even after the wind, in silence, among books, it has a voice,
in the fields near Kenmare I heard it,
a song full of grief, an utterance of curlews, a single drop

of rain sibillating to the ground when the storm had passed.
Whoever sat behind this frame
was master of that quiet, brought music from nothing,

felt the strength of the tree itself, passing
the pulse of the air to his wrists,
turning his hands to the blurred gold of strings.

Power like this yet it cannot stand by itself.
It needs the forward lean, the crooked arms
the face warmed by firelight, the listening.

So much strength to need the arms of the weak!
So much affection to stop its falling,
to hold it warmly, snugged to the shoulder.

To feel, between the last string and the forepillar
that fierce and impenetrable curve
where we know the sound was sown as though it were a seed.

To know as we hear it, the exact place the sound rested
as it grew inside the ear
and became a tree again, waiting for the ear to waken

to the first impossible note
until silence grew on the tree
and with glad hands we plucked its fruit from the wild air.

[VIII]

THE RIVERS OF DELIGHT

'WHO WAS PREPARED FOR THIS—
WHO WAS PREPARED FOR THIS!'

After Robert Sund

Marvellous lines! Knowing that no one
could be prepared for this
deep golden nut of delight in the center
of things.

Right here, in front of us.
surprised by this feeling,
only a moment's pure attention.
only the lines becoming our own.

Who would have thought of this—
Who would have thought of this!

SEEN FROM ABOVE

Seeing from a high window
the three years old boy
caught by sunlight,
peeing in the garden,
I am suddenly aware
why those small statues abound
gracing our squares and piazzas!

The form is eternal delight,
and the source of that
long golden arch of urine a blessing
of curved tummy and bended knees.

Hands clapped on bottom,
eyes concentrated somewhere
between source and target,
amazed, enraptured,
and miracle again,
the golden line between
subject and object made clear
whose author
transcending duality
looks out at a world
intimately
experiencing his arrival.

THE TASK AT HAND

As I sit here writing
The boys outside are stacking wood.

There is the sound of split rounds
thrown into an empty barrow,

dropped on bricks, thrown against the wall,
dropped on the floor and thrown again.

There is the heavy thud of stacking,
the light click of arranging,

a symphonic cacophony of chit-chat,
shouted advice, the radio

blasting at a low volume they are sure
I cannot hear.

There are raised voices, subtle arguments,
and laughing, a marvellous

robust and entirely appropriate
four-letter word as the wheelbarrow falls

over and over, down the steps, onto the terrace,
spilling logs, cartwheeling to oblivion.

Faced with this, the page should remain blank
and by God, after much effort, it does.

AUTUMN AT BLENHEIM

The path curves so slightly to the left
overshadowed by still branches, and behind
the enormous bridge, dark wings lift above the trees.

The birds are leaving now as the first leaves fall.
Late afternoon sun makes warmth more precious.
From the arch of light beneath the bridge
sunlight bathes her face.

We remember rain all summer,
the grey procession of days, only the brief
flame of roses to ignite the eye.

By the lake we lie so close to the swans
moving in sihouette, in the misted distance
a man calls his dog, his voice insistent
calling in silence.

A man and a woman are walking above
and like the swans are silhouettes.
The migrant birds are crowding above them
while our son is suckling beside me
his mother's face crossed by light.

Inside I am drinking clear water,
thirst quenched, first drop to last,
limbs stretched, holding the warm sun,
watching the geese turn south.

[IX]

THE RIVERS OF SLEEP

LOOKING BACK AT NIGHT

Having read my son to sleep
and sung to him and pulled his
window shut, my tired eyes

see straight through darkness
and watching the moon
see a white sail on an open sea.

I remember years ago,
how I too could steer my boat
to the dark sea from which I came.

Those nights I felt the night wind
and the black waves stir, the hand appear
that leads the child where eyes can't go,

staring through the misted window
while the light behind lent shape
to visions of eternal presence.

Not of God, but better for a child—
all the things he gave the mind to see,
mountains, the open valley,

streams falling though woodland,
the haunt of eagles whose slow elipses
curved all night over my wakened eyes.

Those nights I knew
there would never come an end
to the hidden things of life.

And the secret they gave to me
was all attention, to give them praise,
enliven them with watching.

I took it for granted, but never lost
the thanks for what was granted,
given, rendered out of nothing

or sometimes, miracle of miracles,
out of something given just
before the eye would rest in sleep.

Now, by the small body of my sleeping son
the hidden river in my chest flows with my son's
and I time my speech to the rhythm of his breath

joining my night with his, singing his night song
as if those waters underground
were secret rivers washing through the soul

bringing out the untold life
which is the steam he'll join in growing old,
in silent hours when his sureness

of his self recedes. There he'll find
the rest between the solid notes
that makes the song worthwhile.

The night between the days
that give the lighted hours a form and grace.
-So may he find the light enters

what the night has brought
and he be given entrance to that rest,
gladdened and quiet with breath

until the pale house
swells with light, morning is come
and the faith he has in nights fulfilled.

THE WILLINGNESS TO REST

In my tiredness
  and willingness to rest
    I slipped so far down

I felt the earth
  embraced me
    and knew me once again.

I became
  compressed by earth
    a single drop of water

Slipping through
  small crumbs of soil
    to an earthy darkness

    where my breath unbound.

In those deep
  soils of rest
    I fell again

unbinding more
  to those strange
    pathways

where many waters
  meet in slow descent
    to the place in meeting

where we rise again
    becoming in the spiral rise
        this longing for the surface.

Out of shallow springs
    I float into the first
        hours of night.

Becoming as I leave
    slow streams and ponds,
        a haunt of lilies, and so become

again the unknown child
    looking for a gift
        to give his mother.

All night I work,
    dreaming, hands in the water,
        harvesting the white flowers of sleep.

[x]

THE RIVER HOME

WORKING WITH THE WORD

Walking in the fields one day
I felt the voice of things lean down, in silence,
ask me to speak of what I knew.

I bent down, picked a small grey stone,
felt its cold in the palm of one hand
and slowly in prayer, joined it with the other.

But even that small test I failed
and for long years now
must work with the word of the land.

ONE DAY

One day I will
say
the gift I once had has been taken.

The place I have made for myself
belongs to another.
The words I have sung
are being sung by the ones
I would want.

Then I will be ready
for that voice
and the still silence in which it arrives.

And if my faith is good
then we'll meet again
on the road
and we'll be thirsty,
and stop
and laugh
and drink together again

from the deep well of things as they are.

THE GEESE GO SOUTH

I sit on the wood bench
of a late September day
watching the mountains and rivers
feeding the sea where we live
while over the fence
the sound of a child playing flute
fills the air with calm round notes.

In the distance
purple ridges stretch
north and south
while the waters of the Sound,
still and reflective
part in silence
for the passing boats.

Down by the water
the geese unfold their wings
raise their beaks
and lift into the sky.
Flying up and down
they close together
an arrow of love to the south
and disappear.

We can see and write
with calm articulation, and still,
as night comes
we do not know what we are,
the calm waters will not speak,
the fine glow on the far Cascades
fills the soul but will not tell.
The Saratoga Passage
curves north and south
leading us like geese
northward or southward
for enormous distance
and also keeps its silence.

Are we Afraid?
And the geese,
have they left forever,
their wings beating,
leaving us in winter?

We are not afraid,
though there is much to fear
and we know
there is winter beyond this day
everything I know
flies through the blown sky
of my coming death
to say

we are like those geese
who will land
on the calm shore at last.
We shall have the firm earth,
the earth that holds,
the sky everlasting
and the turn
of every season,

and where
we fold our wings at last,
the mountains, the rivers,
and all the far off lands
will fold in too.

CLOUD-HIDDEN

This chapter is closed now,
not one word more
until we meet some day
and the voices rising
to the window
take wing and fly.

Open the old casement
to the lands we have forgotten,
look
to the mountains and ridgeways
and the steep valleys,
quilted by green,
here, as the last words fall away,
the great and silent rivers of life
are flowing into the oceans,
and on a day like any other
they will carry you again,
abandoned,
on the currents you have fought,
to the place
you did not know
you belonged.

And just as you came into life
surprised
you go out again,
lifted,
cloud-hidden
from one unknown
to another
and fall and turn
and appear again in the mountains

not remembering
how in the beginning
you refused
to join,
could not speak of,
did not even know
you were that
deep
calm
welling
almost forgotten
spring
of eternal presence.